The Irish Handbook for Success and Survival

The Irish Handbook for Success and Survival

By Bill Hickey

iUniverse, Inc.
New York Lincoln Shanghai

The Irish Handbook for Success and Survival

All Rights Reserved © 2003 by Wilfred J. Hickey

No part of this book may be reproduced or transmitted in any form or by any means, graphic, electronic, or mechanical, including photocopying, recording, taping, or by any information storage retrieval system, without the written permission of the publisher.

iUniverse, Inc.

For information address:
iUniverse, Inc.
2021 Pine Lake Road, Suite 100
Lincoln, NE 68512
www.iuniverse.com

ISBN: 0-595-31259-4

Printed in the United States of America

This book is dedicated to all of the Irish, everywhere, but especially to Chicago's Southside-Irish from Bridgeport to Beverly.

I also want to thank my family, my grandparents for coming to America, my mother and father, my wife, my sons, my grandchildren, my brothers and sisters, my aunts, my uncles, my nieces and nephews, my cousins (too numerous to count), and all of my Southside-Irish neighbors, co-workers, and mentors. I love you and thank you all for a great life. With your help, I have succeeded and survived.

"For them it is a disgrace that we are Irish."
—**Saint Patrick**, writing of Ireland's enemies. Circa…451 AD Erin.

"For us there is honor…in that they are Irish."
—**Bishop Cody**, speaking of the newly elected President and other Irish-American war heroes. Circa…1961 AD New Orleans.

Contents

Introduction xi
CHAPTER 1   Being Together and Contributing 1
CHAPTER 2   A Mother's Unconditional Love 3
CHAPTER 3   Courage and the Potato 4
CHAPTER 4   Dynasties and Dreams 5
CHAPTER 5   Motivation—That Inner Drive 6
CHAPTER 6   Seizing Opportunities 8
CHAPTER 7   Carpe Diem 9
CHAPTER 8   Acceptance Is Not Enough 10
CHAPTER 9   Wise and then Wealthy 11
CHAPTER 10   The Pope or the Potato 12
CHAPTER 11   The Free Athlete 14
CHAPTER 12   Irish Herds 15
CHAPTER 13   Happy Ending 17
CHAPTER 14   Goals or Dreams 19
CHAPTER 15   Have a Dream 21
CHAPTER 16   Persistence—a Loving Perseverance 22
CHAPTER 17   How is not Important 24
CHAPTER 18   Big Dreams and Small Plans 26

CHAPTER 19	Pray and Wait	27
CHAPTER 20	Irish Security	29
CHAPTER 21	Health and the Hot Toddy	30
CHAPTER 22	Less Anxiety—More Peace	32
CHAPTER 23	Reduce Your Wrinkles	33
CHAPTER 24	The Pledge Is Not Enough	35
CHAPTER 25	Stir Your Blood	36
CHAPTER 26	Left Brain—Irish Brain	38
CHAPTER 27	Being Irish	40
CHAPTER 28	Leprechauns and Angels	41
CHAPTER 29	Heroes Are Everywhere	43
CHAPTER 30	Everyone is a Teacher	44
CHAPTER 31	The Gift of Gab	45
CHAPTER 32	Keep your Head in the Clouds	47
CHAPTER 33	Find Your Gift	48
CHAPTER 34	Share With Everyone	50
CHAPTER 35	Winning with Power	51
CHAPTER 36	The Lesson of Galway Bay	53
CHAPTER 37	Master Yourself	54
CHAPTER 38	Doubt and Fear	56
Conclusion		59
About the Author		63

Introduction

This book is about the success and survival of millions of people, the Irish-Americans and how you can use their traits, experiences, and examples to not only survive, but to succeed. This is not another book about the elite few who made it, how they made it, and how you too can copy six-or-so magic things that they did to become rich and successful. This book is not about the elite at all.

The Irish, Chicago's Southside-Irish, the Boston Irish, the New York Irish and all of the other Irish across our country have built a new society in America.

The elitists, the establishment, have, in the past, done everything in their power to keep the Irish down. Some would say they are trying to keep the Irish from "ruling the world." The Irish do not want to rule the world. The Irish do not want any of the things the elitists are fiercely protecting.

The Irish do not take what others have; they build their own. They have built their own churches, their own schools, their own universities, and hospitals. The Irish have educated their own doctors, scientists, and professionals in every field.

Nor are they separatists; they share all of this with everyone because they know from their past how it feels to be left out

This book is about not only success and survival, but it is also about being open, being together, and sharing what each of us has to offer the other. For example, the chapter on teachers says in essence, "Everyone is a teacher." This chapter not only talks about how the Irish tend to learn from everyone, it also talks about being inclusive, excluding no one, being open to everyone, and sharing what they know.

The chapter on winning is about how to win without being contentious. Use power, not force, to reach your dreams. One of the models in this chapter, Mayor Richard M. Daley, is a living example of winning over and over again. He is winning not only elections, but also the day-to-day political victories and compromises necessary to run a great city like Chicago.

Most of the chapters contain examples of the experiences, teachings, and traits of my Irish mentors, neighbors, and relatives.

This book talks about the characteristics and traits the Irish developed through their experiences and some of the traits they were born with due to, I think, the experiences and challenges their ancestors lived through in Ireland.

My hope is that, as you read this book, you will see that many of these traits can be adopted and used in your day-to-day struggle to succeed and survive. I also hope that you can learn other unstated lessons from the Irish experiences and examples presented in the book.

I hope that you will use this book as a handbook, a resource in your daily life. Further, I hope that you might even carry the book with you as a reference to guide you past the challenges that arise in pursuit of your dream on a day-to-day, hour-by-hour basis.

Many people tell me that I glamorize, romanticize, and make the Irish experience more exciting than it really is. Maybe I do. If I do, then I say "read on, join me." Then you can have not only success and survival, but also glamour, romance, and excitement in your life.

1
Being Together and Contributing

With a box of marshmallows and a bunch of dry twigs, my mother would start a yard party. At dusk, she would have me and my brothers gather twigs and make a big pile of them in our front yard. She would have us shove dry leaves under the pile of twigs. Then she would set the leaves on fire. The flame from the leaves and twigs would reach five to six feet into the air. Within minutes, every kid in the neighborhood was in our yard. We had a gathering, a yard party. My mother brought out the marshmallows and we sat around the fire for hours, telling jokes, laughing, and enjoying each other's company.

The Irish are a gregarious people. They love to be with each other and with other people. Find areas with even a small segment of Irish in it, and you will find an area that is warm, friendly, and open to all. There will be holiday parties and summers barbecues; and in places like Chicago, block parties, park picnics, downtown concerts, and events that the whole city is invited to.

The Irish love these gatherings; this crowding together is part of who they are, and where they come from: a small island of eight million people. Most of them grew up in large families with three to thirteen-plus children, usually living in a relatively small house. They are used to crowding together. For most of them, this is a natural, comfortable, and joyful place.

Thriving in such crowded spaces, they grow up to be very social adults. They like people. They want to be around them. They want to contribute to their well being. Thus, when the Irish join a company or a profession, they bring with them this positive approach to others. The number one incentive is not pay, benefits, or working conditions; it is "what can they contribute?" If the answer is "plenty," they want in.

Once the Irish move into a field, they start contributing—not only to their immediate enterprise, but also to the industry or profession as a whole. The Irish want to share their successes with everyone. Thus, they are contributors to industry round table discussions, trade journals, professional papers and books. A random review of trade journals in my office indicates Irish-American contributors to the trade journals are about 20% to 40% of all contributors. The most current trade journal in my office, *Registered Representative*, May 2004 lists the top ten contributors to the financial advisory profession for the year 2004. Four out of the top ten contributors are Irish-American. The Irish want to share. The more they share the more they grow and the more the enterprise grows.

This is what industry and professions want; they want large contributors. They want people who are willing to share their knowledge, ideas, and talents with others. Be a helper, a contributor in your work and in everything else you do.

2

A Mother's Unconditional Love

My mother was Irish, Catholic, and the mother of nine children. She loved everyone and everyone loved her. To her, it seemed, love was something you gave without condition. She was the personification of unconditional love. She was the center of our lives.

In many movies and books, the Irish mother, especially the Irish-Catholic mother, was portrayed as a sad, overworked, male-dominated, childbearing, mere shadow in the Irish family. The outside world saw her as a lonely and hard-working woman who spent her life in the service of others, and then died at an early age.

However, Irish-Catholic children will tell you a different story. They will tell you of a woman dedicated to her family, fierce in its defense, and determined to keep everyone together. She loved all her children passionately and unconditionally. The Irish will tell you that their mothers were the embodiment of unconditional love.

Contrary to being lonely, the Irish-Catholic mother was surrounded by people who loved her dearly. She kept a home and hearth that everyone wanted to gather around, from the very young to the very old. When people gathered in her home, many, especially the young, stayed until the early hours of the morning and left then only because she suggested, "it was time to sleep." The sharing of joy and story telling always ended reluctantly, usually with a final conversation at the front door tying up loose ends.

Because of this unconditional love freely given, most Irish mothers live well into old age. They are sustained, supported, and surrounded by love. Irish mothers are given every reason to live. After they pass on, they continue to live in the minds and hearts of those who love them.

The unconditional love of the Irish mother is the model of love that you can carry in your heart, and in turns, pass on to others. Then you, too, will attract the love, joy, and friendship of those around you.

3

Courage and the Potato

Courage has played an important role in Irish history. The Irish farmer was in a constant struggle to bring in the next potato crop and he usually succeeded. However, in the 1840's the crops were sometimes much less than expected.

Then "Black '47," hit them. In 1847, the potato crop, a staple food for the Irish, failed them completely. Many Irish peasant families ate potatoes three times a day. It was all they had.

In the face of this killing famine, millions of Irish were literally starving to death. Summoning up ultimate courage, they left Ireland, their homeland, their farms, and everything they knew.

With their courage "screwed to the sticking place," they boarded sailing ships and immigrated to America, coming at first by the hundreds of thousands and finally, when the potato crops and relief efforts continued to fail them, they came by the millions. Over two million Irish drummed up the courage to leave their homes, board death ships, and seek work, food, and shelter in America.

Courage comes from inside. You can call it up with a prayer. You can call it up with a song. You can call courage up, as my mother taught us, with a thump, thump, thump: simply place your fist over your heart and while thinking of your God, your higher power, your spirit, strike the area over your heart three times. Do this repeatedly until you feel the courage within you rising. Do it again when you feel your courage waning.

Courage is the key to everything. Say a prayer, sing a song, and drum it up, thump, thump, thump!

4

Dynasties and Dreams

The Irish are not interested in dynasties. They are not interested in having power or permanently controlling any segment of society. Each place the Irish have been has been a step   reams.

When John   t, the press was full of commentary that this   the Irish would perpetuate and strengthen for   ould reign on. The Irish had no such intentio   nnedy's death. It was because Kennedy's ele   nt one, but still for the Irish, just part of the jou   , to another place where they can contribute.

Shortly after Kennedy's election, some Irish were already beginning to shift from voting straight Democratic, to voting for persons on the ballot who appealed to them regardless of party. Some Irish for the first time in their lives were voting for Republicans. In the years that followed, instead of building on the Kennedy victory through the Democratic Party, the Irish continued to vote more independently, that is, "split ticket" voting, as we call it in Chicago. In 1980, Mayor Daley warned Jimmy Carter, the Democratic candidate for President, that the Irish-Catholics, especially tradesmen, were favoring, and would probably vote for Ronald Reagan. Ronald Reagan, the Republican, won the election and became America's fortieth President. The Irish were on to their next step and looking for candidates that they felt would be supportive and sympathetic to their new agenda. To paraphrase President Kennedy, "They were on their way to another place where they can do for their country."

Dynasties are outer-directed and ego serving. Dreams and destinies are inner-directed. Dreams feed your spirit, your heart, and your soul. Be inner-directed, guided by your inner voice telling you what is right and what is wrong and where the next step is.

5

Motivation—That Inner Drive

The Irish are people of action. They are always doing something: moving, creating, and working. They believe it is *action* that creates motivation. Action leads the Irish to move to the next task. They believe they will be led to the next step once they start doing something. As I said earlier, the Irish first arrived in the United States in large numbers because of the Irish Famine of 1847. Once in America, they were jammed into ghettos and they took some of the most dangerous and lowest-paying jobs available, often because that is all they could get. Eventually they decided they needed to take social and political action if they were to change their working and living conditions.

They had no master plan; they were poorly organized. However, they soon began organizing through their churches and local political organizations. The Irish workers began demanding more pay and better working conditions. They went on strike against the railroads and other industries that were exploiting them. They won small victories and built on them.

They organized local labor unions, then whole industries. One of the first industries they focused on, the mining industry, had some of the worst working conditions. They helped organize the United Mineworkers, led by John L. Lewis. Later they initiated the merger of the AFL and CIO, at that time led by George Meany. The successful merger made the AFL/CIO a giant and powerful labor organization that arose from relatively small groups of determined people who acted.

Actions by the Irish attracted and motivated others to join them. This led to greater and greater successes. The Irish acted both individually, and as a group, inspiring one another to further action. They are now, as always, moving, creating, and working; they are acting.

Let action lead you to higher and higher levels of motivation. Motivation has been defined by Webster as "an inner drive that causes a person to do something." You can bring this inner drive into your life by acting. (See Chapter Ten)

6

Seizing Opportunities

When the Irish first came to America, they were scorned, thought of as lazy, ignorant and in general—especially the Irish men—not good workers.

History has proven these myths and opinions to be unfounded. The truth is the Irish were and are some of the hardest workers in the world. They would take any job and do it well. Why? First, of course, they needed the basics of life: food and shelter. Second, they wanted the self-respect that came with work. Finally, they knew that no matter how lowly society deemed the job, from work came opportunity. Opportunity has been defined as "a chance for advancement."

The Irish have become and are still experts at seizing opportunities. In fact, they are legendary gatherers of opportunity, because they saw the value of action.

In the construction industry, the Irish took any job they could get usually the lowest of laboring jobs available. They were the pick and shovel workers. They did those jobs well. They were then moved into assistant to tradesmen positions and other more skilled jobs. They saw opportunities to become tradesmen. They became some of the best tradesman in America, our carpenters, bricklayers, and electricians. Soon they were the foremen. Now, they are the owners of many of America's construction companies. The Irish are the major builders of America.

Many people call this "the luck of the Irish." The Irish call this seizing opportunity, their chance for advancement. They saw that each job they took, each action they took, and each move they made led them to further action. Action after action led to greater and greater opportunities.

They saw early on that the best way to uncover opportunities is through action. It leads you to do the next thing.

If you are looking for opportunities do not rely on luck, start with action. Do something! Opportunity will show up. You will see your "chances for advancement."
(See chapter five.)

7

Carpe Diem

The Irish are dreamers. They dream about tomorrow, and how good it will be. They reminisce about yesterday, and how good it was, but they know today is the day. Today is the day in which they will be creating their successful past and their promising future. Today is the day that counts. They only have this day, this hour, this minute. "Sure and what else do you need?" my cousins, The Higgins would say.

You should know your dream. Know in general where you are going, what you want to do, and why. Then each day, pursue your dream. Do the things necessary in this day to move closer and closer to your dream.

Do not look back except for positive reinforcement about your successes. Do not dwell on mistakes. There are no mistakes, only lessons learned, things we know that do not ⬛ focused. Outsiders call it denial.

Press on. Live ea⬛ay count. Each day take at least one more step ⬛ member, you do not have a time limit; the deadl⬛

Do not look too ⬛h, may be as far forward as you can clearly see. ⬛ing into the mist, guessing and making yoursel⬛ really have only now, this hour, this day in which to act.

Know your dream. Pursue it steadily and with a loving perseverance. Never look back, except for lessons, and do not look too far ahead. Press on. Work in the present, the now. Make today the day that counts. Carpe Diem! Seize the day.

8

Acceptance Is Not Enough

In 1961, the newly elected President John F. Kennedy came to Chicago's McCormick Place to thank Mayor Richard J. Daley and his political army for his election victory. I was part of that army.

McCormick Place, then the largest meeting hall in Chicago, was packed with thousands of supporters of the new President. It was an Irish celebration. Tickets to the event were $100 a piece, a huge sum at that time. Yet, demand for the tickets was so great that there were people outside of McCormick Place offering us up to $300 for a ticket. "What will you take for your ticket?" they asked, pleading with us to give up our tickets. There were no sellers.

Mayor Daley introduced the new President. John Fitzgerald Kennedy stepped to the podium and looked over the huge crowd. There was a silence. The hall was as quiet as a baby's bedroom at naptime. The President leaned into the microphone and whispered, "Thank you." Then in an emotional, conversational tone he said, "Thank you." Then he leaned back from the microphone and shouted, "Thank you Mayor Daley. Thank you all."

We rose to our feet, applauded, cheered, and hollered with glee for what seemed like five or ten minutes. Some of us had tears of joy in our eyes. This was a grand and proud moment in our Irish-American history.

John F. Kennedy was elected President. The most powerful man in the world was Irish and he was Catholic! We now had the acceptance and approval of our fellow Americans. Was this not enough?

For most of us, it was not enough. While it was a grand and proud moment in our history, it was not the end. It was not something we were counting on. It was outside of us. We depend on ourselves, on our internal spirit, our soul, not on any one political party, or person, not even completely on our church.

Acceptance and the approval of others may be important as the next stepping-stone in your life, but it is not ultimately significant. Internal acceptance is true power. Love, peace, and joy come from within.

9

Wise and then Wealthy

When you grow up Irish and Catholic, you are constantly told and instructed to do the right thing. Obey your mother and father. Do what the nuns tell you. Be nice to your brothers and sisters. Follow your Catechism and, of course, the Ten Commandments.

Much of this emphasis on the right thing I believe, comes from our ancestors. They have been defending Ireland from invaders for hundreds of years. Their strength, their endurance, their ability to prevail in the face of larger armies and tremendous force of arms is because they are doing the right thing: defending their home, their land, and their religion from armies bent on murder, plunder, and pillage.

The Irish race has hundreds of years of training in doing the right thing under chaotic conditions. Thus, the Irish know by instinct what is right, what is good, what is the right thing to do, and they have passed that trait on to subsequent generations.

Great strength, great endurance, great energy is built by doing the right thing. This behavior sweetens your wisdom and ultimately this behavior, in America's land of opportunity, can make you wealthy.

Doing the right thing will lead you to sweeter wisdom and greater wealth.

10

The Pope or the Potato

An English politician once asked, "In the matter of the Irish problem, what is our attitude? Is it the Pope or the potato we are fighting about?" This Politician's attitude was that the English were superior, "good." The Irish were inferior, "bad."

He obviously did not know that in the matter of attitudes, it is best not to have one. Next best is to have a much-diminished attitude in the face of most circumstances.

A strong, set, negative, or positive attitude can lead to immediate rejection or acceptance of a person, place, or thing without considering its merits or faults.

Your immediate responses due to set attitudes could be:

This is good—This is bad

This is pretty—This is ugly

This is black—This is white

There is no thought as to merit or fault; your response is led by your attitude in each example. On the other hand, an open or diminished attitude, one of, "I wonder what this is like," could open a world of new experiences for you.

This diminished attitude, this openness, allows you to choose thoughtfully your response to each person and each situation you encounter. In this mode, rather than proceed on automatic, you can choose how you respond to someone of say, a different race, a different religion, or from a different side of town. Bad feelings are diminished or may not be present at all. Fear may be replaced by wariness, a ste[...] be replaced by tolerance. Attraction may be re[...]k, "Is this really a dangerous person? I wonder [...]ey as good as they look?"

Try not to have a set attitude of this is good—bad—pretty—ugly—black—white or at least, have a much diminished one, one set of circumstances at a time. This openness can lead you to new experiences. These new experiences can widen your world and lead you to more and more learning with less and less fear, hatred, and resentment.
(See chapter Thirty-three)

11

The Free Athlete

The Irish have struggled for centuries to be free. They are attracted to unrestricted, free behavior. They were probably some of America's first free athletes.

The free athlete is the person who trains, builds stamina, strength, and athletic ability, not for external gain, but for reasons important only to him or herself. For example, while 40,000-plus people participated in the 2003 Chicago Marathon, only small fractions were professional athletes running for the money, the product endorsement contracts, and other rewards. Thirty-nine thousand-plus participants were free athletes, people running for their own internal reasons, for their dreams.

If you asked them why they were running, you would get thousands of different answers. Every dream, like every person, is somewhat different.

Most free athletes are not concerned about where they are positioned in the pack, what the route is, or even where the finish line is. They are aware of these factors, but the important criteria, the measures they count, are internal, in their hearts, in their souls, where their dreams are kept.

The free athletes follow no pacer, they are not that concerned with who is in front of them, who is gaining on them, and they know there will be no tape to break when they cross the finish line. They are free athletes. Their measures are not on any clock or milepost.

The free athlete trains, participates, and dreams. It is not about money, prestige, and awards. It is about being fit, having endurance, being healthy, resilient, and being free.

Be a free athlete.

12

Irish Herds

Although we were very poor, I grew up thinking I had potential. I thought I could be whatever I wanted to be, because my father and my mother said that to me over and over again. "You hav⬛⬛⬛⬛⬛⬛⬛⬛pirit. Nothing is holding you down. You can be ⬛⬛⬛⬛⬛⬛ould say.

The lower fields of life, the th⬛⬛⬛⬛⬛⬛⬛are monetary, tangible, and visceral. You may ⬛⬛⬛⬛⬛⬛⬛don't have a dependable car, I don't have the ⬛⬛⬛⬛⬛⬛⬛To overcome the steady grasp of the lower fiel⬛⬛⬛⬛⬛⬛⬛it and higher power of life and your potential. ⬛⬛⬛⬛⬛⬛⬛alone in this world. The power that brought y⬛⬛⬛⬛⬛⬛⬛ays will be. If you do not believe in your potential and the power of your soul to lead you, you will never move away from where you are.

For some people, it is like being in the middle of a herd, inside a fence. I believe that there are two types of herds, the Ordinary Herd, and the Irish Herd.

The Ordinary Herd

The ordinary herd sees a fence around them with a gate that is always open. However, few people seem to either notice or care about the open gate. Indeed, most will deny that there is a gate. Their fate, their destiny, is all lived inside the fence, in the middle of the herd, because they ignore the open gate.

The Irish Herd

The Irish herd sees only parts of a fence. Most do not even notice the parts. Many will deny that there is a fence at all. The Irish control their own fate, their own destiny, and their own lives. For most of them, there is no gate because they see no fence.

Believe in the power of your heart, your soul, and your spirit to lead you to your full potential.

To paraphrase an old Irish ditty:
> *Control your own fate.*
> *See no fences, see no gate.*

13

Happy Ending

The Irish no longer dominate the Southside of Chicago as they once did. Many of us have moved to other areas. Some moved to the suburbs, some moved to the north side of Chicago, and some to other states, other cities.

The point is, as we went forward step-by-step in our careers, we sometimes found it necessary to move, to leave our old neighborhoods, our parishes, our friends, and relatives. Some of us moved to be closer to our new work and new opportunities that we saw in other areas that we were now qualified to pursue.

These moves always took courage. We had to sell our homes, leave everything we knew behind, and move to a place we did not know, and worse yet, usually no one there knew us.

My family and I moved to the suburbs. We moved from a close-knit family oriented city neighborhood to a new suburb. In the city, we lived on what we considered a large lot. It was fifty feet wide. In the suburbs, the lot we lived on was a whole acre of land. It was almost two hundred feet wide. The home was a big white house, like the house on Tara, from *Gone with the Wind*. The adjustment period was long. The center of our old neighborhood for most people was family. The center of our new neighborhood for many people was golf. However, with time, courage, and perseverance we did adjust and we did succeed and survive in our new home.

We adjusted by seeking out and becoming friends with people involved in golf but who were also focused on their family. With our new friends we met with the police chief in our area and became involved in a teenage drug prevention program. We took the program to higher levels. I began giving speeches to local groups as part of our fund raising efforts. We used the money to hire an outside speaker to talk to the students at a huge anti-drug rally during the day. That night, after the student rally, we again packed the school gymnasium for the parents program. As the master of ceremonies, I introduced our outstanding speaker. He was a sensation. The audiences loved him. The program was a success.

Suddenly, we were known and knew many people in our new neighborhood and, most importantly, we were involved and contributing.

If you want to get to where you are going, you too may have to call up your courage, and leave your old neighborhood and everything you know behind. You may have to start a new job, move from the country to the city, or go back to school. You should be prepared to move or to do whatever it takes, in pursuit of your dream.

14

Goals or Dreams

Goals

Dreams are flexible, but a goal must be stated, should be written, can be measured, and has a time limit. If you are goal driven, once your goal is fulfilled there is a vacuum; another goal must be put in its place.

For example, your goal is to have $25,000 in a savings account within three years. You work nights and weekends and give up friends and parties. You do not go anywhere, do not do anything else but sleep, eat and work for three years.

Finally, you accomplish your goal. You have $25,000 in the bank. Now you do not need to work the extra time, but you have hardly any friends, you have no place to go, and nothing to do. You feel let down, useless, but you met your goal. You now have time, energy, and resources. Now what do you do? You set another goal.

On and on and on it goes goal, fulfillment, emptiness; goal, fulfillment, emptiness; goal, fulfillment, emptiness.

Because of this cycle of goal, fulfillment, emptiness, most people, especially, the Irish go with dreams.

Dreams

This chapter and the opinions in it are written from direct personal experience. I worked as an executive in a goal driven corporation. After three years, I resigned. The environment was too rigid and had no spirit, no joy. I left. I moved on, to do the Irish thing, follow a dream.

A dream can be written, but usually it is not. It cannot be measured and has no time limit. It is usually never completely fulfilled. It can last a lifetime and beyond.

Your dream could be to build a business that is profitable and good to its workers and customers. You live your dream, day-in, and day-out. You make many new friends, you go to many places you had not even dreamt about, and you have many interesting experiences. You sleep, eat, and live for your dream and all the people in it.

Now, at the end of three years, you are living your dream. You have many friends, you have many places to go, and many things you could do. You feel joyous and useful. You have time, energy, resources, and the support of good friends. What do you do? You keep living your dream.

On, on, and on it goes. Dream, joy; dream, joy; dream, joy....

15

Have a Dream

The Irish are dreamers. We love our families and each other dearly. We know what is important and what is significant in our lives.

Dreams and meaning come from the intangibles in our lives. Meaning comes from the love in our lives, our souls, what we value. Meaning comes from our spirit. It tells us what is important and what is significant. You are empowered by what you stand for, what you create. For example, I am an artist, I am a tradesman, and I am a _____. You fill in your own blank. If you rise to the occasion, you are the creator of your own life.

By supporting your dreams and what you stand for, you are creating your life and life for the supporting players who are attracted to your spirit, your meaning, and your dream. Through attraction and hard work, those who follow you will rise too. The tide, your meaning, lifts all boats, raises all dreams, your dreams and the dreams of those around you.

A recent study indicates that fifty-seven percent of Americans have no dreams, thirty-five percent are not fulfilling their dreams, and only eight percent are. You say you have no dreams, that "nothing turns me on", that there is no meaning in your life. Then go with that, start working with "nothing." That is where creativity starts, from nothing, a blank page. Before it was passed to the engineers and the politicians for building, "The Irish Freeway," the Kennedy Expressway between O'Hare Airport and Chicago, was a dream. It had its start as a blank page on the desk of a dreamer, someone who thought maybe we can find a faster, better way to get from Chicago to O' Hare Airport.

Start searching; discover the meaning in your life by determining what you value. By knowing what you value, you will know what is truly significant to you. Knit these two together and create your dreams, your career, your place, your highway.

Live your dream; fulfill it, action-by-action, step-by-step, and day-by-day. Do not live without a dream.

16

Persistence—a Loving Perseverance

Persistence comes naturally to the Irish, especially those who are pursuing their dreams. For those pursuing their dreams, persistence is not a stubborn tenacity, but rather a loving perseverance. They continue day in and day out in the direction of their dreams despite challenges that may arise.

This loving perseverance is best expressed by a line from a popular Willie Nelson song, "You are always on my mind." The thought of your dream, persistently, continuously, stays on your mind like a sweet melody, a haunting love.

An example of this in my early life was my mother's dream. My father had moved us from Chicago to rural Indiana, because he could not afford the rent in the city. My mother's dream was to move back to Chicago. Her family, her mother and father, sisters and brothers were all in Chicago. She loved her family and they in turn loved her and all of her nine children.

My mother always had her dream on her mind. She mentioned it often, especially to me. Everyone in her family knew she wanted to be back in Chicago. Then one day, unexpectedly, "out of the blue," as we would say, an opportunity appeared. I was now sixteen and working in Chicago. After work one day, I stopped to see my Aunt Mamie, my father's sister. I loved visiting her. She was tough but one of the sweetest, warmest, most caring persons I ever knew. She too loved my mother and all of her children. She said to me, "I hear your mother wants to move back to Chicago." I said, "Yes. Three of us, my brother, my sister, and I are working and giving her money. She feels she can afford to live in the city again."

My aunt smiled and said, "Good. Your great aunt is living alone in a large house, just a few blocks west of here; she's elderly and needs some day-to-day help. She only lives in a small part of the house. Your mother and dad can move you all into her house. Then, you can help her, take care of the house for her, and make your mother happy all at the same time."

I rushed home to tell my mother the news. She was so happy. Of course, she cried for about an hour. Within weeks, we moved into my great aunt's house. My mother's dream had come true. She was back in Chicago. All she ever did in pursuit of her dream was to talk about it and keep it always on her mind.

Be naturally persistent in the pursuit of your dream. Maintain a loving perseverance in the face of the challenges in your life.

Like a haunting love, have your dream "always on your mind."

17

How is not Important

The Irish will tell you that the word with the most power to shatter dreams is "how," as in, "How are you going to do that?"

Mean-spirited people are called "dream-breakers." Tell them your dream, and their first remark is usually, "You can't do that." Then, "That's impossible," etc. If none of the usual put-downs work, they will come up with the ultimate dream-breaker, "How are you going to do that?"

Most of us will not have an answer to that question. Many of us have not even considered the question of "how"; therefore, we sit there unable to reply. We [...]ate. Why had we not thought about "how?" [...]ow" because deep in our subconscious, we know [...]w" will come to us. In any case, the "how" is not [...] higher powers in our lives. You do not need the [...] we have a worthy dream, that we will attract the [...]y to make the dream come to life. We know that

Here is one of the many ways this works. John Hayes, an Irish-American, dreamed of becoming a homebuilder. He knew that he could build houses, but he was not sure he knew how to sell them. He told his wife, Karen, his dream. She was concerned too, so she asked, "How are you going to sell the houses once you build them," John replied, "I don't know yet."

A short time later Karen started a new job in a real estate office. She noticed that Lou Stephens, a top salesperson in the office, was a hard worker, seemed to care about the business, and was selling vacant lots to builders. She told Lou about her husband's dream of becoming a homebuilder. Then she said to Lou, "He needs a good sales person to help him. Would you be interested in talking to John?" Lou, not being Irish, and not then knowing the power of dreams said, "No!"

That night Karen told John about Lou Stephens and the conversation that she had with him. John said, "That's it. He is the guy. We are on our way. I will come in to your office tomorrow. You introduce me to this Lou." Karen said, "OK…but he doesn't want to be a builder." John replied, "He wants to be a builder. He just doesn't know it yet."

John went in to the office the next day and talked, and talked, and talked with Lou. Weeks later, they became partners. Today, they are Stephens and Hayes Construction Co., Inc., one of the largest and most successful homebuilders in the Chicago South-Suburban area.

If a dream-breaker asks the question, "How are you going to do that?" Your ready answer should be, "I don't know yet." Remember, you do not need the "how" in order to have a dream. The "how" will come to you.

18

Big Dreams and Small Plans

I am the owner of an accounting and financial advisory practice. Over the years, many people have come to our practice with their ideas and their dream for a small business.

People with the dream of starting their own business seem to attract dream breakers. The critics are everywhere. Some potential business owners bring them with them to their meetings with us. "She has no real plan," is usually the first thing a dream breaker says to us. Many times the person with the dream also says to us, "I have no real plan, but this is what I want to do." Then they tell us their dream, and we start from there. We ask, "How much money do you have?" We think, "That's not enough." We do not say it. Instead, we talk further about the dream and how we can get it started. We ask, "Can you borrow money, take on a partner, or sell something to raise more cash, start smaller?" These are the "hard parts" of the dream, the critical decisions that need some resolution so that the dream can go forward. We work with the person on these critical areas. We believe in dreams.

Most of the people we are working with on a daily basis are living their dreams. They are successful business owners, living a sometimes glamorous, sometimes romantic and always an exciting lifestyle.

Plans are necessary schemes for doing day-to-day, week-to-week, sometimes month-to-month things that support your dream. Beyond that time span, on a personal level and on a small business level, most plans are at best a guess at the future. Again, dreams have no time span: they can last a lifetime and beyond.

Go with dreams. Have small plans and big dreams.

19

Pray and Wait

If you have a challenge in your life that is not being resolved, one that appears it may not be resolved, or it may end in tragedy, try the Irish—Pray-and-Wait solution.

When I was a little Catholic boy, my family and I were always praying for something. Our church had us pray for sick classmates, dead parishioners, the farmers' crops, the end of the war, and of course the salvation of our souls.

Closer to home, my mother had more personal, more family things to pray for. She had us pray a lot. Many days in the summer time, she would call us in to pray the Rosary with her. We would all kneel down beside her and pray the five decades of the Rosary. We prayed aloud. "It was better that way," she would say. To this day, when I pray, if I can, I pray aloud.

Many of the times when we prayed with my mother, it was "for her intentions," she would tell us. Other times my mother's prayers were for more specific things, her mother's health, one of my aunts getting a much-needed job or the safety of my cousin in the Navy. She always said to us "all we can do is pray and wait."

At other times, it was extremely critical and very urgent, that is, we had a crisis, and we needed help now. One of these crises occurred when I was about four years old. My five-year-old sister Dolores was very sick. The doctor and my mother talked at the bedroom door. The doctor said she was dying. Then, he called my brother Jim and me over to the door. He told us, "Go into the bedroom and kiss Dolores goodbye."

The doctor's tone frightened me. I did not know what "dying" meant, except that he told us that we would never see Dolores again. I peered into the room: it was very dark. My little brother Jim was the physically braver of the two of us so I pushed him in first and followed him. We said our good-byes, kissed our sister, and came out of the room.

My mother took us into the front room of our apartment, and we knelt down and prayed. We prayed and waited. We prayed and prayed and waited and waited.

My sister did not die.

Try the Irish-Pray-and-Wait solution for the challenges and crises in your life. Remember, when you can, pray aloud, "it's better that way."

20

Irish Security

Looking for security, many of Chicago's Southside-Irish, including the author, became civil servants in the 1940's, 1950's, and 1960's. However, most of us quickly realized that this was not real security. Many of us eventually resigned. We were reminded by this experience that security comes from inside, from the soul, the heart, and from courage.

If you are a civil service employee, or have tenure or seniority, you may think you have security but that is not real security. Real security comes from depending on yourself, your talents, and your gifts, not on your employer.

Real security is knowing that no matter what happens, no matter who does what, no matter what breaks down, you can carry on. To gain security you need a focused and near-reckless hand guiding you through life.

Today, change comes at blinding speed. Just a few years ago most of us wrote letters on a piece of paper and/or typed it and mailed it out. Today letters, documents, and whole books are entered on computer keyboards. Then they are, in many cases, not mailed, they are E-mailed! Daily, you find yourself pouring over this change and many other changing circumstances and adapting. The leaders, the winners, and the survivors make change and circumstance their slaves, their advantage, and their tools of success. They never bemoan a change and say, "Why did this have to happen?" They adapt to it, work with it, or move on, being sure to never let it gain control of them.

Do not depend on your job or other tangibles in your life for security; build security from within. You must know that, no matter what happens, you can carry on. You must maintain a focused and near-reckless hand in guiding yourself to success, survival, and constant growth.

21

Health and the Hot Toddy

As I said before, we lived for many years in rural Indiana. The nearest doctor was 5 miles away. There were not many people in the area with dependable cars. Therefore, when you were sick, you were usually on your own. We only had each other to turn to for help. You were usually given a home remedy. If you lived in our house and if you had a cold and fever, my father would be your self-appointed doctor. He would mix up a Hot Toddy for you to take as a medicine. A "Hot Toddy" was a cup of strong tea, a good dash of whisky, and a spoonful of brown sugar all mixed together. Then the concoction was brought to a boil and allowed to cool only enough to be able to drink without burning yourself. You were then told, "Drink it, stay in bed, get plenty of rest, let my father, the 'doctor,' know how you were doing every morning, and you would get better." That was it. It was up to you, my father, the Hot Toddy, and the bed rest to make you better. Amazingly, you usually got better.

If health is a problem in your life, you too may have to turn to yourself for relief. You may have to take charge. You may have to monitor your doctor's advice and watch how the medicine she prescribes is working. Watch how your body and mind are reacting to it. Constantly ask yourself, "Is it working? Am I getting better?" Make daily notes on how you are doing and review them with your doctor.

You can also help yourself and your doctor by watching what you eat. Know what foods are good for you, especially during a healing process. Do not take any food for granted. Just because it is on the recommended list of an expert, does not always mean its best for you.

After each meal, each snack, each drink, ask yourself, "What is my physical reaction here? How is my body handling this, with harmony, with easy digestion? How's my energy level? Rising, falling? What is my psychological reaction? Is the food causing an emotional reaction: a so-called sugar high, depression, some change in feelings or behavior?"

Be certain that each time you eat food and drink a beverage that their effect on your mind and body is at least neutral, at best positive. In other words, watch what you eat and monitor its effect.

If health is a problem in your life, you may have to help yourself. You should keep your doctor informed on how the medicines are working and how you are progressing. In addition, you should watch what you eat and how it is affecting you. Keep in mind that this is an on-going, constant endeavor, and can be a life-giving, lifetime process. Remember, also, that you are ultimately the person responsible for your health.

22

Less Anxiety—More Peace

Your mind is like a lake caught in the wind. The faster the wind blows over the water, the higher the waves on the lake. The faster thoughts race through your mind, especially negative thoughts, the higher the anxiety level you reach. Anxiety has been defined as "worry about what *may* happen." To slow the thoughts in your mind and lower your anxiety level, consider meditation. It is better than drinking and has no negative side effects. "You don't have the bad head in the morning."

Meditation has not been a widespread Irish practice. However, it is important. Meditation, in its simplest form, is noting and dwelling on the space between the noise of the thoughts that race through your mind. Meditation, in general, for me, is an attempt to quiet my mind, make the spaces between the thoughts longer. It's calming yourself down, moving to a peaceful mode, and holding it. If you feel you cannot meditate, just go for the small spaces between the thoughts in your mind.

Find a place where you can go to and deliberately think nothing. At first, try for tiny spaces, seconds, or even milliseconds between thoughts and then work for wider gaps. Do not measure these gaps. This is not a contest. You are just seeking peace through the gaps.

Once you establish some meditation skills, some ability to quiet your mind, you will begin to feel more in control of your life, more peaceful, less and less ego-centered, more accepting, and more loving. You will be more aware, more energized, and yet more relaxed. You will be more in tune with the motives of others, the reasons, and drives that lead to their actions.

Calm yourself, quiet your mind. Gain more control over the thoughts running through your mind. Use meditation to lower your anxiety level and move to a more peaceful place in your life.

23

Reduce Your Wrinkles

Stress is like a sail on a boat that is lofting, fluttering, because it is not with the wind. A full sail is in harmony with the wind. It is not fluttering. Indeed, it has no wrinkles in it at all. It is smooth and sending you speedily over the water. You can reduce your stress, that is, take the wrinkles, the fluttering, out of your days and have harmony in your life.

To remove most of the stress in your life, try this Irish power: make a list of everyone with whom you are angry. Add to the list everyone you hate, who misunderstood you, rejected you.... Wait now—take a deep breath, exhale, this is not one of those Irish lists of people you are going to punch out. This is a list of people with whom you are going to make peace.

Make a complete list. Then, one by one forgive the people on the list. See them, visualize them, and then let them go. Let them go completely, graciously, with no resentment, no contempt, and no reservations.

Do this because accepting people as they are, forgiveness, understanding are purging. It makes you feel clean and healthy. It leaves you lighter, stronger, and free.

Listed below are other Irish traits that you can adopt and use to reduce stress:

> Do not try to control or change what has happened. Instead, work to influence what will happen as you go forward.
>
> Know that your life has purpose and meaning. If you do not see the purpose in your life, search for it. You may never find the final purpose, but there is much joyful distraction in the searching. Ask yourself, "Why am I here?" without a need for an immediate answer.
>
> Believe that love is at the center of your life. Cherish the things you love, keep them in sight, and close to you. Shower the people you love with expressions of your feelings with looks, words, and hugs. Let them constantly know of your love and your caring. Expect nothing in return except the inner joy your generous and intense love radiates.

Reduce stress; take the wrinkles out of your sail. Fill it with harmony. Make your list. Forgive everyone on it. Work to influence your future. Bring meaning into your life. Cultivate a generous and intense love for the people around you. Forgiveness, less control, meaning, and love will make you feel cleaner, lighter, stronger, and healthier, and you will have more harmony and less stress in your life.

24

The Pledge Is Not Enough

Because of the addictive quality of Alcohol, my family and many other Irish families have struggled with the difficult process of one or more family members recovering from alcoholism. This process takes time and steps. Fifty years ago, a popular Irish treatment for alcoholism was to appear before a priest and pledge not to drink again. This was called, "taking the pledge." At my mother's request, I took my father to the Parish Priest many times to take the "pledge." However, this one old-time Irish treatment does not work.

If you and your family are faced with the challenges posed by alcoholism or drug addiction, you must see that with God's help and the help of others, you can recover. Bravery, determination, and courage must be summoned.

You must constantly remind yourself you can do this with the help of God, your groups, your family, your coaches, and your readings. You are growing stronger minute-by-minute, hour-by-hour, day-by-day. That is why they call it recovery. It is not easy, but when you recover, you are rewarded. You get to be you, who you were meant to be. The fog lifts; you can see again.

What do you need to do to get started? Take one action, then another. One action, one little positive action will move you to the next. Alcoholics Anonymous calls the actions "steps." How does this work? Each step moves you higher and higher and higher, in faith, in spirit, and in hope, step-by-step, day-by-day. To start recovery for you or someone in your life, one of the first steps you might take is to call AA, Alcoholics Anonymous or NA, Narcotics Anonymous

One day you and your family look down and see you are not where you were. You are in a new place in your life. You are above the fog. You can see again, and most importantly, you can see a future. You have hope again. You have stopped stumbling through life and have started deliberately stepping from place to place.

25

Stir Your Blood

My nephew, Michael, got married to the beautiful Julie. It was a typical Southside-Irish wedding with lots of joy, love, friendship, reminiscing, food, and drink. After a full dinner, the hall got a little quieter. The guests were settling down and relaxing. At some of the tables, the story telling was beginning.

Suddenly, there was a great stir at the large entrance doors to the hall. In marched the Shannon Rovers, a Chicago based Irish BagPipe Band. They played for about thirty minutes. They played *Danny Boy, When Irish Eyes are Smiling, Toora-Loora-Looral* (a salute to Irish mothers) and many other Irish songs. By the time they were through playing almost everyone was on their feet. The guests were singing, clapping, and dancing to the music. They were energized. The noise level rose and the party started anew.

The pipes are an Irish legend. They stir our blood and inspire us. The Irish love the bagpipes. The pipes led out ancestors into battle. Irish soldiers always carried music with them, especially the pipes. They can hear music over the roar of battle. It reaches the fighters; it inspires them. It tells them when to charge, when to hold, and when to retreat.

As you work with this book, try to find the music that goes with what you want to accomplish. Find music that will draw you into your current activity. When you turn on the music, it should evoke a Pavlovian response; you immediately start moving towar⬛⬛⬛⬛⬛⬛⬛⬛⬛⬛ "Everybody Has a Dream," may immediate⬛⬛⬛⬛⬛⬛⬛⬛⬛ ınd get you moving toward it.

If you have a personal⬛⬛⬛⬛⬛⬛⬛⬛⬛ ned for yourself, that you have decided to do e⬛⬛⬛⬛⬛⬛⬛⬛⬛ eed inspiration to get started, have music that⬛⬛⬛⬛⬛⬛⬛⬛⬛ an move you, inspire you; make you want to ⬛⬛⬛⬛⬛⬛⬛⬛⬛ ın energetic marching band or a hot little jazz g⬛⬛⬛⬛⬛⬛⬛⬛⬛ exercise program, and the time will pass quickly and joyously and have you looking forward to the next session.

To help with your inspiration, try to anchor music to as many activities as possible in which you are involved. Then, turn on the music and all else will follow.

26

Left Brain—Irish Brain

Most of my Irish friends and family members and I tend to be mainly dependent on our right brain for decisions in our lives. We are so called right brain people, that is, more subjective in our thinking. The left-brain deals with scientific, systematic knowledge. It helps you determine how things work. The right brain works with intuition and feelings. It helps you determine how you work.

Knowing which side of your brain is activated, which side is dominating your thinking will help you know if your decisions are going to be objective or subjective, practical or romantic, rigid or flexible.

If you are dealing with a relationship, and you find yourself thinking rigidly in black and white, you may want to adjust your thinking to rely on your right brain. You may want to allow some flexibility, some romantic and subjective factors to help you along. However, if you are planning a road trip from Chicago to Miami, you may want to be more left brain and practical in your plan. You will want to think more linearly, more step-by-step, town-by-town.

I know from my own experiences that you can make a major change in your life by making slight changes in your thinking on a subject. The changes in the example that follows resulted from the process I used in gaining my college degree.

I started with the left brain, the practical side. I said to myself, "I could read some books on the next step in my career." I did that. Then I move to, "I could take a course on the next step in my career." I start with a small change, and allow it to lead to another change.

Once I saw the effect of the small changes, then, with the holistic right brain, I suggested to myself, "I should make my next dream a college degree program. The degree would qualify me to move to the next level in my life, closer to my destiny." Thus, by starting with a small change, major changes started coming into my life.

Try to determine which side of your brain dominates you. Are you inclined to be objective, practical, and rigid? If you are, try to work in some subjectivity, some glamour, some romance, and some excitement into your life.

Remember, if you have a problem with change; try to change by taking small steps, little by little, through the left brain. Once you see progress, then try conceptual, larger changes through the right brain.

Then, perhaps one day you will look up and see that your whole life has changed. You no longer are who you were. You are rising higher and higher, step-by-step in the area of your life you wanted to change.

27

Being Irish

Once every two weeks, my mother would go to her mother's home for the day. She would leave me in charge of the family, seven children at that time. She would say, "You are responsible."

I was 11 years old. I took responsibility. I watched over my brother and sister and made certain that nothing bad ever happened while she was gone.

You, too, should try to be responsible for nearly everything in your life. All right, you are not responsible for everything that happens to you. After all, stuff happens: stuff like accidents, random weather events, and earthquakes, things over which you have no power. However, you are responsible for how you react to these events.

I, like many of my Irish mentors, have always tried to be the responsible person, the person people call when they are in trouble or faced with a challenge, the person people would call if they were allowed only one phone call. For many of us, in our minds, being Irish is being responsible.

Imagine, you are being held and allowed only one telephone call. Whom in your life would you trust with that one call? Who do you know that would come and get you? Do you know anyone whom you could call? Many people do not. They do not have anyone whom they could trust, someone who would be totally responsible, and would come to free them.

There are not many people out there who are responsible in both personal and business life. If you want a role in life, if you want to fill a vacuum, being the responsible person, the "go to guy/gal," is the place to be. If you can be this person, then friends, co-workers, relatives, and some people you barely know will flock to you, gather around you, and be supportive of you.

Be Irish; be responsible. The more responsible you are, the more secure the people around you will feel. If you are there for others, in the long run, they will be there for you.

28

Leprechauns and Angels

Ireland is a place of spirit, a place of leprechauns, angels, and saints. The Irish believe in the spiritual world. They in turn have passed this spirituality on to us, the Irish-Americans.

Irish-Catholic children of the 1940's, 1950's, and 1960's were raised in a spirit-filled world. We each had a guardian angel. We had the saint we were named after to watch over us. We had the Saint our school and church was named after to guide us. We had Jesus' mother, Mary, to help us and keep us from evil. We were protected. We knew how to pray. We were spiritual. At least that is what we believed. In fact, most of us have carried this spiritual tendency into adulthood. We want this same feeling, this feeling that we are not alone. We want the feeling that with the help of the angels, the saints, and the Holy Family we can accomplish great things. We are inspired.

You can be inspired too. You do not need to become a Catholic or accept all of the beliefs we were raised with. You only need to accept the definition that being inspired means being in spirit and further that being in spirit is having meaning in your life, a meaning that causes you to take action, move mountains, and do the right thing. Then you will look to the future with hope, with what you might do. You will look to today with what you can do. You will look at the past with the joy of what you have done.

Here is how you can have meaning and build spirit in your life:

- Have a Higher Power you love
- Have a dream you love.
- Have people you love.
- Have places you love.
- Have things you love.
- Have memories you love.
- Have hopes you love.

Be inspired in spirit; nurture these qualities. You do not need to tell anyone about them, but share them with everyone through your actions and your spirit.

29

Heroes Are Everywhere

You should have heroes in your life, people you look up to; people you can emulate, and people who inspire you. My personal hero, as a child, was my Uncle Jimmy, James Hickey, killed on a battlefield in Europe during the Second World War. A little later, my hero was my cousin Fran, a United States Marine.

More recently, my heroes have been closer to home, my family and mentors. These people helped me, supported me, and encouraged me as I moved step-by-step, higher-and-higher in my life.

They helped me find my courage when I began to think I had little or none. They are the people who gave me their time, their energy, their faith, and in some cases, their money, especially in the years when I was in college. They ask for nothing in return. All was given unconditionally. Some of these heroes were of another persuasi[...]re not even Irish.

Now more th[...]d we are still sharing.

Look for her[...]d, an aunt, an uncle, a cousin, a local police o[...]r, your co-worker, heroes are everywhere.

You should [...] **and people in your life that you can count** [...] **can emulate and copy, when necessary. The** [...] **you, and cause you to reach higher and higher in pursuit of your dream.**

30

Everyone is a Teacher

The Irish, especially my mother, have a belief that says, "Everyone is a teacher. You can learn from everyone." The teacher is not always dressed in a tweed jacket.

If you accept this concept, you are going to include some interesting, unusual, and difficult people in your life. Many of your teachers are going to be very interesting. They will be doing things of great importance, usually in an efficient and productive way. They may be writers, builders, entertainers, or politicians. They keep your attention just by the fact that they are doing things that interest you.

However, some of your teachers are going to be strange, hard for you to identify with and figure out. They will not dress like you, act like you, nor do many of the things about which you care. You may want to dismiss them as not important to your learning. Stop and ask yourself, "What can I learn here? Why am I dismissing this person? Is it prejudice? Is it because they are not my 'kind'?" I hope that one of these questions will cause you to pause, look, listen, and possibly learn what this strange person has to teach you.

S/he may be one of the best teachers of all. This type of person may be a challenge, but s/he can teach you humility and patience and bring knowledge to you that "ordinary" people do not have.

Indeed, in corporate America, it has been proven over and over again, the person who can work and grow with unusual, strange and talented people is often the most successful.

Everyone is a teacher. You can learn from everyone.
(See chapter 36)

31

The Gift of Gab

The Irish are talkers. Many have even traveled to Blarney Castle to kiss the Blarney Stone. Legend has it that kissing the stone gives you the gift of eloquent speech; in other words, you get the "Gift of Gab." However, I think the Irish are talkers because they are also, good listeners. They know that conversation should be a two-way exchange. When in a conversation, they focus on the other person and his/her words.

Let us assume you and another person are in a friendly conversation that the other person started. As you begin, immediately move to a state of compassion. Get into an "I want to understand," mode. Try to determine what the other person is talking about; what s/he is saying point-by-point. Let the other lead. You will not know where s/he is going if you keep pulling the conversation in your direction. Follow the 70/30 rule: the other person talks at least 70% of the time, and you respond 30% of the time.

Try to maintain eye contact. Show interest, but do not stare. If the other person seems uncomfortable even with a moderate amount of eye contact, then nod more often to indicate interest. In fact, no matter what level of eye contact you maintain, nodding at those points with which you agree is very positive for both you and the speaker.

Keep yourself focused on the speaker. Mirror his or her body language: sit in the same fashion: lean as s/he leans, and hold the same facial expressions. This will enable you to understand the speaker better, more easily feeling what s/he is feeling, knowing more fully his or her pain or pleasure.

Convey expressions of empathy, "I know what you mean, Wow! How did that happen? Say that again!" Try to get closer to the deeper meaning of what the speaker is saying. Be earnest and non-manipulative.

Avoid any hint of being competitive. Do not think, "How can I match that?" or worse yet, "How can I top that?" To insure that the other person walks away feeling good, give them the last word.

Among the conversational skills, there is one that is more important than the others. It is the key to giving the other person a feeling of the power of your understanding. It is this, if you think of something you would like to say in response to the other person that might draw attention to yourself, or if it would be self-serving even to the slightest degree, don't say it. Delay your comment for another day.

Get the "Gift of Gab" for you. When you are in conversation be compassionate and understanding. Try to determine why the speaker is talking, and what points s/he is making. Allow the other to lead; follow the 70/30 rule. Maintain consistent eye contact, nod to show your interest, and:

Stay focused on what they are saying.
Mirror their body language.
Try to feel what they are feeling.
Convey expressions of empathy.
Do not try to top the speaker.
Never make self-serving responses
Give away the last word.

32

Keep your Head in the Clouds

Most of the succeeding and surviving Irish are optimists. We are accused of having our head in the sand. We say, "we have our head in the clouds." We have lots of hope. We expect that not only will things work out, but, also, that things will get even better. Our dreams will come true. Senator John Kerry said of Former President Ronald Reagan, "He always left you with the feeling that things were going to get even better."

Life has constantly gotten better. The U.S. government economists tell us that they expect that our standard of living will double over the next thirty-five years. Our life expectancy continues to rise. On and on the good news goes. There is enough good news to encourage hope. "There are lots of things to hang your hopes on." The Southside-Irish would always say.

You too should have a lot of hope—a never-ending supply of it. Where your dreams are concerned, you can never have too much hope.

Have hope that your energy will carry you through. Have hope that your talent, your specific ability, your aptitude, your gift from God will not only be there, but will also carry the day for you. Hope that your talents will move you to the next step and hope you will bring whatever vitality you need to the work at hand.

Always be optimistic! It stimulates your talent, your energy, and your intellect. Hope will carry you through the darkest nights and sail you speedily through the brightest days. Expect that things will work out and get even better for you. Expect that your dream will come true. Remember, you can have your head in the sand or you can have your head in the clouds, it is up to you.

33

Find Your Gift

Everyone has a gift.

A young Irishman, Babe Ruth, barely ten years old, stood at the plate in a schoolyard with his bat-in-hand. This was his first time up. The other boys in the yard were taunting him, calling him names, and laughing. The priest in charge threw him a pitch. Babes swung, met the ball squarely, and boom! The ball soared out of sight. The taunting and laughing stopped. The other boys stood stunned, in awe, and amazed at what they had seen. That quickly, Babe Ruth discovered his advantage, his gift, and his talent.

Everyone has a gift like Babe Ruth's. Yours may not be as great and you may have to search for it.

Almost everyone, who excels, is truly great, and a big contributor to the world, talks of his or her gift. It is not all them; there is something else, something given to them, some major strength, insight or talent, a gift.

How did they acquire this gift? They went out looking for it! The search usually begins by working for excellence in some area of endeavor. For some it is in the arts, entertainment, a profession, trade, or small business. They are usually pulled to their area of interest by intuition, a strong hunch, and/or their dream.

Once they start their search, they look for their advantage, their opportunity. Then, usually, slowly, they realize they have a talent, an ability, some part of the endeavor that is coming to them easier and faster than to their peers. Once they start working with it, it starts to grow in power, advantage, and importance. They get the feeling, "Maybe I can do something with this."

If it begins to look better and better to them every day, if the more they work with it, the larger, the more significant it becomes in their lives, they have found their gift.

Start the search for your gift. Find your opportunity, your chance for advancement, and your advantage, the thing you do better. Find the place where you excel, your gift.
(See chapter 10)

34

Share With Everyone

Saint Patrick was given the gifts of extreme devotion to his God and high intellect. He shared these gifts with everyone. With his love of God, the Saint ordained priests, converted, and baptized thousands of Irish into the Christian faith. With his love of learning and his high intellect, he was able to educate priests and build monasteries and other shelters where these newly educated clerics could gather the people in their area and pass on their knowledge.

Like Saint Patrick, once you find your gift, modest or great, love it, nurture it, and never exploit it solely for personal gain. Share it with everyone. You share, not by bragging about it, but by using it for service to others. By helping others, you and your gift grow stronger and stronger.

The more you share your gift, the more support you will receive from others. The more you use your gift to be of service to others, the more people you will attract to your dream. Sharing will make you more exciting, more attractive, and more inspiring as a leader and a person.

Saint Patrick was gifted, kind, and generous. He shared his devotion and intellect with everyone. More than 1540 years after his death, people around the world still celebrate his life.

Share your gift. Use it for the benefit of others. Nurture and grow your gift. This will attract others to you and inspire them to begin their search for their advantage, their excellence, and their gift.

35

Winning with Power

Forcing, trying to make something happen, is unnatural. Force is constantly fading in strength, and needs continual reinforcement. Power, the power of inner strength, especially power based on equality, on the Golden Rule, constantly grows, becomes stronger and stronger, rising on its own. Power is doing the right thing. Force is "the end justifying the means."

Typically, the power of inner strength does not arouse resistance. If it does, the resistance, the opposition, finds little place to attack, to have an effect. Power, like a river running down a mountain, takes great energy and resources to stop. Even then, once you stop a mountain stream with a dam, it merely keeps flowing until it spills over the top.

A living example of power, of Irish political power, is Chicago's Daley family. Mayor Richard J. Daley was mayor of Chicago for 21 years, and now his son, Richard M. Daley, has been mayor for more than 14 years. When either campaigned, they were always the predicted winner and appeared to win without great effort.

They had a distinctive style. They did not run negative ads; they did not attack their opponents, and they refused to debate. A debate would surely subject them to attack and force them into counter-attack. They, the mayors Daley, would campaign in the right way. They would promise to do the right things when elected, and then when they were elected, they did the right things. With this campaign and governing style, they gathered many friends and supporters and few detractors. Many times, the opposition would run only a token candidate, if any, against them. The mayors Daley would win and win over-and-over again by large margins. Incredibly, nobody seems to copy their style.

To have winning in your life, do the right thing. Strive to find what that is; what is right for your dream, for your campaign, for the people in your life, and for the people in your dream.

Let the opposition do the attacking. Let them spend the time and energy to build dams. You, with your power, your inner strength, just flow over the top.

Use power in your life. Never, ever use force. Never argue with opponents. Stay on your point, not theirs. Make this your style.

36

The Lesson of Galway Bay

The British have tried for hundreds of years to control the people of Ireland. These efforts by the British to dominate the Irish have led to tragedy after tragedy. The Irish have set these tragedies to music. In "Danny Boy," a proud mother laments her son being called to battle against the British. In "Grace," an Irish-Catholic prisoner says good-bye to his love, because he will be shot at dawn.

On a personal level, the need to control another can also lead to tragedy. You can, it seems, only control another person for short intervals, if that. Even then, you cannot be sure he or she is doing things your way or just pretending. You cannot get into the individual's head to determine what s/he is truly thinking. In the song, "Galway Bay," controlling another is like trying to "light a penney candle from a star." You are going to get burned.

Yet, over and over again, people try to control another. This effort to control usually stems from a need for the approval of the person over whom control is being attempted. Between a man and a woman, it is sometimes the near constant need of the man to know that the woman loves him.

This type of domination is classic. It is the basis of many modern novels and love stories. It usually starts with the man saying, "I love you. Do you love me?" and the woman replying, "Uh, Yes." If the questioner sees the "yes" as tentative or not as positive as he would like, the tragedy begins. If he feels he does not have the approval of his love, he starts exerting control. He tries to determine where she goes, who she sees, what she does.

If this form of regulation fails, and it usually does, then measures that are more violent come into play: screaming, restraining, hitting, and sometimes beatings that escalate to the tragedy of death itself.

Try to let go of the need to control another. Remind yourself that your desire to control is usually rooted in the need for approval. Let go of the idea that security comes from another person. Give up your demand for approval; free the other person, free everybody, and you free yourself.

37

Master Yourself

While control of another is impossible, control over yourself is possible and may be the most rewarding dream you can pursue.

You win the small battles over control one at a time. You can, in the words of Tolstoy, "Master yourself." Like any battle in which control is a factor, you want satisfaction, you want approval, and you want it known that you are doing a good job. Gaining self-control, a large or even a small amount of it, gives you that pleasure.

For example, people who quit smoking have gained a tremendous victory and exerted great control over self. They have also given themselves the gift of improved health, stamina, and a sense of satisfaction and self-approval that they will carry with them for the rest of their life.

Make controlling yourself easier, less arduous, and less stressful by making the control you seek a dream, not a rigid goal. Control should not be something you are imposing on yourself. To make things even easier, enlist the help of others. Get support from self-help groups, people close to you who love you and truly want to help with this control, this dream. You need these others, the people who are striving for the same dream as yours. They know what you are going through. They know how to help and most of all; they are mirrors for you. They are doing what you are doing, and in some cases, have achieved some measure of success. Some may have the control that you are seeking. Mirrors, mirror images, people with the same challenge, the same dream, and people who have accomplished the dream, give you hope and a living example that this control, this dream can be achieved.

With greater self-control, you will gain satisfaction, self-approval, and the feeling that you are doing well and in control of you.

Make the control you seek a dream. Enlist the help of others. Have mirrors; they really work.

In the matter of control, my father said it most succinctly, "Never mind your brother, control yourself."

38

Doubt and Fear

Saint Patrick wrote, "For them it is a disgrace that we are Irish." The enemies of Ireland had murdered many and kidnapped some of his followers the day after they were baptized. He wrote further, of the victims, "the fragrance was still on their foreheads."

Despite these dangers, at the urging of Saint Patrick, many of the Irish people let go of their doubts and fears and continued to follow his teachings. The Saint's teachings were not only on the value of the Christian religion but also, on the value of practical learning. The clerics and other teachers the Saint educated, taught the Irish to read, write, and to understand basic mathematics. These clerics and teachers also educated and trained others to carry on their work. With no doubt and little fear, the Irish people were able to follow the dream and the teachings of the Saint into "The Golden Age of Ireland."

You too must have no doubt and little fear. You should watch for doubt and fear because when they move into your life, you may stop following your dream. Instead, you may find yourself moving quickly to the "how" mode of thinking. You start asking yourself, "How can I get out of this? How can I get away from here? How will I get enough money to pay for this?"

You should be focusing back on your dream. Look at it, think about it, and visualize it. See it happening, being accomplished. Then your next step, despite the current challenge, will come to you. You will see that there are things you can do now to move forward, move closer to your dream.

Once you start focusing and doing what you can do, you see progress, you see certainty and courage coming back into your life. Doubt and fear fade away. Years later you will look back and think, "How did I ever see that little bump on the road to my dream as such a mountain?"

Try this, depending on your age, think back to when you were 10…16…25…35 years old. Try to remember what was causing you great doubt and fear at these ages. Can you remember anything? Most of these doubts and fears have probably faded away. Those that you do remember will probably make you smile and think, "That seemed so important then, but now it's past. I made it through. It is over. I am in a new place, and I am stronger." All of those past doubts and fears were just misplaced, misdirected energy. You moved on to where you are now, closer to your dream.

Watch for doubt and fear in your life. If it happens and you find yourself in the "how" mode, focus back on your dream. You should act. Do whatever you can do to move closer to accomplishing your dream. Then you will see progress, certainty, and courage coming back into your life. Doubt and fear will start fading away. Soon you will be free of them, free to move closer and closer to your dream.

If you want to accelerate the process, try this. Shake your head from side to side saying, "No, no, no. I do not doubt myself, my ability, or my courage." Then, nod your head up and down and say, "Yes, yes, yes. I am brave, I am strong, I can move past this." Then, take a deep breath and move on into your "Golden Age."

Conclusion

For a non fiction book to be true to its readers, it must be an earnest and sincere effort by the author to convey and share what he has experienced and learned in his life. This is my attempt to do that for you, to share with you my Irish-American life, step-by-step to success and survival.

Like millions of Irish—Americans, I believe that you too can succeed and survive by adopting the traits, absorbing the experiences, and learning from the examples of my Irish mentors.

Listed below are words and phrases from the book that will help you succeed and survive:

- Contribute to your dreams and the dreams of others.
- Rely on your right brain for dreams and your left brain for plans.
- Learn to talk less and listen more.
- Know that with dreams, "now" is important and that "how" is not.
- Act with great courage and a loving perseverance.
- Be inner-directed and self-reliant.
- Have big dreams and small plans.
- Be free of attitudes, doubts, and fears.
- Find music that moves you and people that inspire you.
- Love unconditionally and forgive almost anything.
- Act and stay motivated.
- Protect your health and reduce your stress.
- Search for your gift and watch for your opportunities.
- Learn from everyone and control no one.
- Be responsible and have heroes.

Finally, believe that:
Life has meaning.
Love is the center of everything.
There exists a good and loving God.
Hope and optimism are your prevailing feelings.
You can accept people and events as they are.
You can and will continue to grow.

Carry these passages with you. They will lead you through the day-to-day challenges on the way to your dream, to your "Golden Age."
Be like the Irish, have glamour, romance, excitement, success, and survival in your life.

Acknowledgments and

Suggested Readings

James Allen, *As a Man Thinketh*
(A classic)
Barnes & Noble Books, New York, 1992
ISBN 0-88029-785-9

David R. Hawkins, *Power Vs Force*
(Revolutionary and powerful reading)
Veritas, 2000
ISBN 0-9643261-1-6

Robert J. Kriegel and Louis Patler, *If it ain't broke...BREAK IT!*
(Unconventional wisdom that everyone can use)
Warner Books, 1991
ISBN 0-446-51539-6

Wayne W. Dyer, *Wisdom of the Ages*
(If you can, read everything he writes)
Harper Collins, 1998
ISBN 0-06-019231-3

Frank McCourt, *Angela's Ashes*
(A story of tragedy, love, success, and survival)
Scribner, 1996
ISBN 0-684-87435-0

Jim Ainsworth, *In the Rivers' Flow*
(A story of family love, tragedy, growth, success, survival, and finding the flow)
Dan River Press, 2004
ISBN 0-89754-196-0

Thomas Cahill, *How the Irish Saved Civilization*
(A bit of history and why we, the Irish, are the way we are)
Anchor Books, Doubleday, 1996
ISBN 0-385-41849

Terry Golway & Michael Coffey, ***The Irish in America***
(A narration of the experiences of the Irish in America)
Simon & Shuster Audio, 1997

About the Author

The author Bill Hickey is a second generation Irish-American. He is the oldest son of nine children. He has lived the typical poor Irish—Catholic life. Over the past 60 years he has moved, step-by-step, higher and higher, in his own pursuit of success and survival. He was a farm worker, a construction laborer, a tradesman (bricklayer), a United States Army First Sergeant, a civil service employee, a college graduate, a corporate executive, and now the owner of two successful businesses.

He has lived his life amazed at the success and ability to survive that people in his Southside-Irish community have exhibited on a day-to-day basis. Many of them have moved literally, from the bottom of society to success and survival.

He, his four brothers, and four sisters lived for many years in a two-room shack, slept sideways on two beds in one bedroom, and received most of their food and clothing from the government.

Later they moved to a five-room shack and received only some of their food and clothing from the government. They considered this a big step up. Somehow, through these times, they were not only able to survive but succeed.

Today, he is the President of Bill Hickey and Associates, Inc., an accounting, tax, and financial advisory firm located in Orland Park, Illinois. His practice was established in 1972. The company serves both individual and business clients.

He is a University of Illinois James Scholar. He graduated with Distinction, class honors, and individual honors. He is an Enrolled Agent, licensed to practice before the Internal Revenue Service.

He was appointed to a National Advisory Board of Tax Professionals. He was awarded the National Professional Assistance Designation and the National Outstanding Service Award. He was appointed to American Funds' All American Team, Scudder Funds' Executive Council, and for continued outstanding service to clients, he was given the Eagle Award by 1st Global Capital Corporation.

He lives in Chicago, Illinois with his wife and family.

His e-mail address is BillHickey@direcway.com.

0-595-31259-4